12-MONTH

MONTH

Undated Student Planner

THIS PLANNER BELONGS TO:

_____

Seek the Kingdom of God above all
else, and live righteously, and He
will give you everything you need.

Matthew 6:33

2024

January
S M T W T F S

February
S M T W T F S

March
S M T W T F S

April
S M T W T F S

May
S M T W T F S

June
S M T W T F S

July
S M T W T F S

August
S M T W T F S

September
S M T W T F S

October
S M T W T F S

November
S M T W T F S

December
S M T W T F S

2025

January
S M T W T F S

February
S M T W T F S

March
S M T W T F S

April
S M T W T F S

May
S M T W T F S

June
S M T W T F S

July
S M T W T F S

August
S M T W T F S

September
S M T W T F S

October
S M T W T F S

November
S M T W T F S

December
S M T W T F S

2026

January
S M T W T F S

February
S M T W T F S

March
S M T W T F S

April
S M T W T F S

May
S M T W T F S

June
S M T W T F S

July
S M T W T F S

August
S M T W T F S

September
S M T W T F S

October
S M T W T F S

November
S M T W T F S

December
S M T W T F S

Identifying
EMOTIONS

funny	happy	sad	disappointed	exhausted
silly	shocked	sneaky	disgusted	confused
unimpressed	loving	playful	ecstatic	unenthused
cheerful	content	relieved	tired	desperate
embarrassed	adoring	neutral	elated	worried

"How to Study Effectively"

Make a Study Plan
When making a study schedule, look at your planner and think about what needs to be accomplished.

Steer Clear of Distrations
Be aware of what distracts you in class and know how to steer clear of these distractions.

Get Organized
Carry a homework planner at all times like entering homework, projects, tests and assignments, etc.

Start Studying More Effectively
Get more out of your study sessions with a complete study toolkit including note taking template, tips, ect.

Designate a Study Area
The best study spot is one that is quiet, well-it, and in a low-traffic area.

Simplify Study Notes
Make studying less overwhelming by condensing notes from class.

MULTIPLICATION

1

1 x 0 = **0**
1 x 1 = **1**
1 x 2 = **2**
1 x 3 = **3**
1 x 4 = **4**
1 x 5 = **5**
1 x 6 = **6**
1 x 7 = **7**
1 x 8 = **8**
1 x 9 = **9**
1 x 10 = **10**
1 x 11 = **11**
1 x 12 = **12**

2

2 x 0 = **0**
2 x 1 = **2**
2 x 2 = **4**
2 x 3 = **6**
2 x 4 = **8**
2 x 5 = **10**
2 x 6 = **12**
2 x 7 = **14**
2 x 8 = **16**
2 x 9 = **18**
2 x 10 = **20**
2 x 11 = **22**
2 x 12 = **24**

3

3 x 0 = **0**
3 x 1 = **3**
3 x 2 = **6**
3 x 3 = **9**
3 x 4 = **12**
3 x 5 = **15**
3 x 6 = **18**
3 x 7 = **21**
3 x 8 = **24**
3 x 9 = **27**
3 x 10 = **30**
3 x 11 = **33**
3 x 12 = **36**

4

4 x 0 = **0**
4 x 1 = **4**
4 x 2 = **8**
4 x 3 = **12**
4 x 4 = **16**
4 x 5 = **20**
4 x 6 = **24**
4 x 7 = **28**
4 x 8 = **32**
4 x 9 = **36**
4 x 10 = **40**
4 x 11 = **44**
4 x 12 = **48**

5

5 x 0 = **0**
5 x 1 = **5**
5 x 2 = **10**
5 x 3 = **15**
5 x 4 = **20**
5 x 5 = **25**
5 x 6 = **30**
5 x 7 = **35**
5 x 8 = **40**
5 x 9 = **45**
5 x 10 = **50**
5 x 11 = **55**
5 x 12 = **60**

6

6 x 0 = **0**
6 x 1 = **6**
6 x 2 = **12**
6 x 3 = **18**
6 x 4 = **24**
6 x 5 = **30**
6 x 6 = **36**
6 x 7 = **42**
6 x 8 = **48**
6 x 9 = **54**
6 x 10 = **60**
6 x 11 = **66**
6 x 12 = **72**

7

7 x 0 = **0**
7 x 1 = **7**
7 x 2 = **14**
7 x 3 = **21**
7 x 4 = **28**
7 x 5 = **35**
7 x 6 = **42**
7 x 7 = **49**
7 x 8 = **56**
7 x 9 = **63**
7 x 10 = **70**
7 x 11 = **77**
7 x 12 = **84**

8

8 x 0 = **0**
8 x 1 = **8**
8 x 2 = **16**
8 x 3 = **24**
8 x 4 = **32**
8 x 5 = **40**
8 x 6 = **48**
8 x 7 = **56**
8 x 8 = **64**
8 x 9 = **72**
8 x 10 = **80**
8 x 11 = **88**
8 x 12 = **96**

9

9 x 0 = **0**
9 x 1 = **9**
9 x 2 = **18**
9 x 3 = **27**
9 x 4 = **36**
9 x 5 = **45**
9 x 6 = **54**
9 x 7 = **63**
9 x 8 = **72**
9 x 9 = **81**
9 x 10 = **90**
9 x 11 = **99**
9 x 12 = **108**

10

10 x 0 = **0**
10 x 1 = **10**
10 x 2 = **20**
10 x 3 = **30**
10 x 4 = **40**
10 x 5 = **50**
10 x 6 = **60**
10 x 7 = **70**
10 x 8 = **80**
10 x 9 = **90**
10 x 10 = **100**
10 x 11 = **110**
10 x 12 = **120**

11

11 x 0 = **0**
11 x 1 = **11**
11 x 2 = **22**
11 x 3 = **33**
11 x 4 = **44**
11 x 5 = **55**
11 x 6 = **66**
11 x 7 = **77**
11 x 8 = **88**
11 x 9 = **99**
11 x 10 = **110**
11 x 11 = **121**
11 x 12 = **132**

12

12 x 0 = **0**
12 x 1 = **12**
12 x 2 = **24**
12 x 3 = **36**
12 x 4 = **48**
12 x 5 = **60**
12 x 6 = **72**
12 x 7 = **84**
12 x 8 = **96**
12 x 9 = **108**
12 x 10 = **120**
12 x 11 = **132**
12 x 12 = **144**

MEASUREMENT CONVERSIONS

LENGTH

Customary Units

1 Foot = 12 Inches

1 Yard = 3 Feet

1 Mile = 5,280 Feet

Metric Units

1 Kilometer = 1,000 Meters

1 Meter = 100 centimeters

1 centimeter = 10 millimeters

CAPACITY

Customary Units

1 Gallon = 4 Quarts

1 Quart = 2 Pints

1 Pint = 2 Cups

1 Cup = 8 Fluid Ounces

Metric Units

1 liter = 10 Deciliters

1 liter = 1000 Millimeters

WEIGHT

Customary Units

1 Pound = 16 Ounces

1 Ton = 2,000 pounds

MASS

Metric Units

1 Kilogram = 1,000 Grams

1 Gram = 1,000 Milligrams

TIME

1 Minute = 60 Seconds

1 Hour = 60 Minutes

1 Day = 24 Hours

1 Week = 7 Days

1 Year = 12 Months

1 Year = 52 Weeks

1 Year = 365 Days

1 Leap Year = 366

Angles & Their Measures

Do you want to build something? Understanding and measuring angles is essential when working with space, whether you want to improve an existing project or start a new one!

rays

60°

vertex

What are angles?

Formed when two rays or line segments meet at a common endpoint called **vertex.**

How to measure an angle using a protractor?

Step 1:

Place the protractor's center point at the angle's vertex.

Step 2:

Align the protractor's bottom line with the bottom ray of the angle at the 0 mark.

Step 3:

Find the angle measure by reading the number where the second ray intersects the protractor.

The angle is 30°

Mastering Angles with a Protractor

The angle is 50°.

The angle is 130°.

Exponent Rules

Exponent of Zero ✕

$$a^0 = 1$$

A base with an exponent of 0 is always equal to 1.

Exponent of One ✕

$$a^1 = a$$

Any number raised to an exponent of 1 is equal to itself.

Exponent of Product ✕

$$a^m \times a^n = a^{m+n}$$

When multiplying exponential terms with the same base, add the powers.

Exponent of Quotient ✕

$$\frac{a^m}{a^n} = a^{m-n}$$

When dividing exponential terms with the same base, subtract the powers.

Exponent of Power ✕

$$(a^m)^n = a^{mn}$$

When a power is raised to another power, multiply the exponents.

Exponent Negative ✕

$$a^{-n} = \frac{1}{a^n}$$

When a number is raised to a negative power, divide 1 by the base raised to the positive exponent.

AUTHOR'S PURPOSE

FOUND IN:

- NEWSPAPER/MAGAZINE ARTICLES
- AUTOBIOGRAPHIES
- NONFICTION BOOKS
- BIOGRAPHIES

FOUND IN:

- POETRY
- FICTION BOOKS
  - FANTASY STORIES

INFORM

When the author writes about a factual topic.

READER'S PURPOSE:

- I LEARNED THAT...
- NOW, I KNOW...

ENTERTAIN

When the author writes about funny, interesting or new topics to keep your attention.

READER'S PURPOSE:

- IT WAS FUNNY WHEN...
- MY FAVOURITE PART WAS...

PERSUADE

When the author writes about something with the intention of changing your opinion to theirs.

FOUND IN:

- NEWSPAPER/MAGAZINE ARTICLES
- ADVERTISEMENTS
- COMMERCIALS
- DEBATES

READER'S PURPOSE:

- I BELIEVE THAT...
- I CHANGE MY MIND ABOUT...

TYPES OF
NOUNS

Proper Noun
Specific names for people, places or things.

A person's name. The name of a place. The name of a thing.

Common Noun
General names for people, places or things.

People: Mom   Place: Park   Thing: Toy

Concrete Noun
Things that you can see, touch, hear, smell, or taste.

Tree. Cat. Dog. Flower. Apple.

Abstract Noun
Ideas or feelings or qualities you cannot perceive with your senses.

Love. Happiness. Bravery. Friendship.

Collective Noun
Groups or collections of people or things.

Team. Family. Class.

Possesive Noun
Shows ownership or possession.

John's car. The dog's tail. The teacher's book.

Countable Noun
Things that can be counted.

Dollars. Classmates. Books.

Uncountable Noun
Things that cannot be counted.

Water. Sand. Knowledge.

SCHOOL YEAR AT A GLANCE

SCHOOL YEAR: _____

JULY

AUGUST

SEPTEMEER

OCTOBER

NOVEMBER

DECEMBER

JANUARY

FEBRUARY

MARCH

APRIL

MAY

JUNE

Commit your actions to the Lord, and your plans will succeed. *Proverbs 16:3*

GOALS:

RPOJECT:

TO DO

- [ ]
- [ ]
- [ ]
- [ ]

- [ ]
- [ ]
- [ ]
- [ ]

IMPORTANT DATES:

BIRTHDAYS:

CLASS/ACTIVITY SCHEDULE
SEMESTER 1

TIME	MONDAY	TUESDAY	WEDNESDAY	THURSDAY	FRIDAY
7 - 8 am					
8 - 9 am					
9 - 10 am					
10 - 11 am					
11 am - 12 pm					
12 - 1 pm					
1 - 2 pm					
2 - 3 pm					
3 - 4 pm					
4 - 5 pm					
5 - 6 pm					
6 - 7 pm					
7 - 9 pm					

CLASS/ACTIVITY SCHEDULE
SEMESTER 2

TIME	MONDAY	TUESDAY	WEDNESDAY	THURSDAY	FRIDAY
7 - 8 am					
8 - 9 am					
9 - 10 am					
10 - 11 am					
11 am - 12pm					
12 - 1 pm					
1 - 2 pm					
2 - 3 pm					
3 - 4 pm					
4 - 5 pm					
5 - 6 pm					
6 - 7 pm					
7 - 9 pm					

Work willingly at whatever you do, as though you were working for Lord rather than for people. *Colossians 3:23*

MONTH:_____

	MON	TUE	WED	THU	FRI	SAT	SUN
WEEK 1							
WEEK 2							
WEEK 3							
WEEK 4							
WEEK 5							

TO TO LIST

NOTES

PROJECT PLANNER

PROJECT TITLE:

OBJECTIVES:

START DATE: . . . .

DEADLINE: . . . .

TASK LIST   DUE DATE

☐ . . . .

☐ . . . .

☐ . . . .

☐ . . . .

☐ . . . .

NOTES

Week Of: _____

Sunday

_____   _____
_____   _____
_____   _____
_____   _____
_____   _____

Monday

_____   _____
_____   _____
_____   _____
_____   _____
_____   _____

Tuesday

_____   _____
_____   _____
_____   _____
_____   _____
_____   _____

Wednesday

_____   _____
_____   _____
_____   _____
_____   _____
_____   _____

Positive Affirmation:_____
_____
_____

Thursday

Friday

Saturday

Notes

Week Of: _____

Sunday
_____ _____
_____ _____
_____ _____
_____ _____
_____

Monday
_____ _____
_____ _____
_____ _____
_____ _____
_____

Tuesday
_____ _____
_____ _____
_____ _____
_____ _____
_____

Wednesday
_____ _____
_____ _____
_____ _____
_____ _____
_____

Positive Affirmation:_____
_____
_____

Thursday
_____   _____
_____   _____
_____   _____
_____   _____
_____   _____

Friday
_____   _____
_____   _____
_____   _____
_____   _____
_____   _____

Saturday
_____   _____
_____   _____
_____   _____
_____   _____
_____   _____

Notes
_____   _____
_____   _____
_____   _____
_____   _____
_____   _____

Week Of: _____

Sunday

_____   _____
_____   _____
_____   _____
_____   _____
_____   _____

Monday

_____   _____
_____   _____
_____   _____
_____   _____
_____   _____

Tuesday

_____   _____
_____   _____
_____   _____
_____   _____
_____   _____

Wednesday

_____   _____
_____   _____
_____   _____
_____   _____
_____   _____

Positive Affirmation:_____

_____

_____

Thursday

Friday

Saturday

Notes

Week Of: _____

Sunday

_____ _____
_____ _____
_____ _____
_____ _____
_____ _____

Monday

_____ _____
_____ _____
_____ _____
_____ _____
_____ _____

Tuesday

_____ _____
_____ _____
_____ _____
_____ _____
_____ _____

Wednesday

_____ _____
_____ _____
_____ _____
_____ _____
_____ _____

Positive Affirmation:_____
_____
_____

Thursday

_____   _____
_____   _____
_____   _____
_____   _____
_____   _____

Friday

_____   _____
_____   _____
_____   _____
_____   _____
_____   _____

Saturday

_____   _____
_____   _____
_____   _____
_____   _____
_____   _____

Notes

_____   _____
_____   _____
_____   _____
_____   _____
_____   _____

Trust in the Lord with all your heart; do not depend on your own understanding.

Proverbs 3:5

MONTH:_____

	MON	TUE	WED	THU	FRI	SAT	SUN
WEEK 1							
WEEK 2							
WEEK 3							
WEEK 4							
WEEK 5							

TO TO LIST

NOTES

PROJECT PLANNER

PROJECT TITLE:

OBJECTIVES:

START DATE: ....

DEADLINE: ....

TASK LIST   DUE DATE

☐ ....

☐ ....

☐ ....

☐ ....

☐ ....

NOTES

Week Of: _____

Sunday

_____   _____
_____   _____
_____   _____
_____   _____
_____   _____

Monday

_____   _____
_____   _____
_____   _____
_____   _____
_____   _____

Tuesday

_____   _____
_____   _____
_____   _____
_____   _____
_____   _____

Wednesday

_____   _____
_____   _____
_____   _____
_____   _____
_____   _____

Positive Affirmation:_____
_____
_____

Thursday

Friday

Saturday

Notes

Week Of: _____

Sunday

_____   _____
_____   _____
_____   _____
_____   _____
_____   _____

Monday

_____   _____
_____   _____
_____   _____
_____   _____
_____   _____

Tuesday

_____   _____
_____   _____
_____   _____
_____   _____
_____   _____

Wednesday

_____   _____
_____   _____
_____   _____
_____   _____
_____   _____

Positive Affirmation:_____
_____
_____

Thursday

_____   _____
_____   _____
_____   _____
_____   _____
_____   _____

Friday

_____   _____
_____   _____
_____   _____
_____   _____
_____   _____

Saturday

_____   _____
_____   _____
_____   _____
_____   _____
_____   _____

Notes

_____   _____
_____   _____
_____   _____
_____   _____
_____   _____

Week Of: _____

Sunday

_____   _____
_____   _____
_____   _____
_____   _____
_____   _____

Monday

_____   _____
_____   _____
_____   _____
_____   _____
_____   _____

Tuesday

_____   _____
_____   _____
_____   _____
_____   _____
_____   _____

Wednesday

_____   _____
_____   _____
_____   _____
_____   _____
_____   _____

Positive Affirmation:_____
_____
_____

Thursday

_____   _____
_____   _____
_____   _____
_____   _____
_____   _____

Friday

_____   _____
_____   _____
_____   _____
_____   _____
_____   _____

Saturday

_____   _____
_____   _____
_____   _____
_____   _____
_____   _____

Notes

_____   _____
_____   _____
_____   _____
_____   _____
_____   _____

Week Of: _____

Sunday
_____ _____
_____ _____
_____ _____
_____ _____
_____ _____

Monday
_____ _____
_____ _____
_____ _____
_____ _____
_____ _____

Tuesday
_____ _____
_____ _____
_____ _____
_____ _____
_____ _____

Wednesday
_____ _____
_____ _____
_____ _____
_____ _____
_____ _____

Positive Affirmation:_____
_____
_____

Thursday

_____   _____
_____   _____
_____   _____
_____   _____
_____   _____

Friday

_____   _____
_____   _____
_____   _____
_____   _____
_____   _____

Saturday

_____   _____
_____   _____
_____   _____
_____   _____
_____   _____

Notes

_____   _____
_____   _____
_____   _____
_____   _____
_____   _____

Never be lazy, but work hard and serve the Lord enthusiastically.

Romans 12:11

MONTH:_____

	MON	TUE	WED	THU	FRI	SAT	SUN
WEEK 1							
WEEK 2							
WEEK 3							
WEEK 4							
WEEK 5							

TO TO LIST	NOTES

PROJECT PLANNER

PROJECT TITLE:

OBJECTIVES:

START DATE: . . . .

DEADLINE: . . . .

TASK LIST   DUE DATE

☐ . . . .

☐ . . . .

☐ . . . .

☐ . . . .

☐ . . . .

NOTES

Week Of: _____

Sunday
_____   _____
_____   _____
_____   _____
_____   _____
_____   _____

Monday
_____   _____
_____   _____
_____   _____
_____   _____
_____   _____

Tuesday
_____   _____
_____   _____
_____   _____
_____   _____
_____   _____

Wednesday
_____   _____
_____   _____
_____   _____
_____   _____
_____   _____

Positive Affirmation:_____
_____
_____

Thursday

_____   _____
_____   _____
_____   _____
_____   _____
_____   _____

Friday

_____   _____
_____   _____
_____   _____
_____   _____
_____   _____

Saturday

_____   _____
_____   _____
_____   _____
_____   _____
_____   _____

Notes

_____   _____
_____   _____
_____   _____
_____   _____
_____   _____

Week Of: _____

Sunday

_____ _____
_____ _____
_____ _____
_____ _____
_____

Monday

_____ _____
_____ _____
_____ _____
_____ _____
_____

Tuesday

_____ _____
_____ _____
_____ _____
_____ _____
_____

Wednesday

_____ _____
_____ _____
_____ _____
_____ _____
_____

Positive Affirmation:_____
_____
_____

Thursday

Friday

Saturday

Notes

Week Of: _____

Sunday

_____ _____
_____ _____
_____ _____
_____ _____
_____ _____

Monday

_____ _____
_____ _____
_____ _____
_____ _____
_____ _____

Tuesday

_____ _____
_____ _____
_____ _____
_____ _____
_____ _____

Wednesday

_____ _____
_____ _____
_____ _____
_____ _____
_____ _____

Positive Affirmation:_____
_____
_____

Thursday

_____   _____
_____   _____
_____   _____
_____   _____
_____   _____

Friday

_____   _____
_____   _____
_____   _____
_____   _____
_____   _____

Saturday

_____   _____
_____   _____
_____   _____
_____   _____
_____   _____

Notes

_____   _____
_____   _____
_____   _____
_____   _____
_____   _____

Week Of: _____

Sunday

_____   _____
_____   _____
_____   _____
_____   _____
_____   _____

Monday

_____   _____
_____   _____
_____   _____
_____   _____
_____   _____

Tuesday

_____   _____
_____   _____
_____   _____
_____   _____
_____   _____

Wednesday

_____   _____
_____   _____
_____   _____
_____   _____
_____   _____

Positive Affirmation:_____
_____
_____

Thursday
_____   _____
_____   _____
_____   _____
_____   _____
_____   _____

Friday
_____   _____
_____   _____
_____   _____
_____   _____
_____   _____

Saturday
_____   _____
_____   _____
_____   _____
_____   _____
_____   _____

Notes
_____   _____
_____   _____
_____   _____
_____   _____

Get the truth and never sell it; also get wisdom, discipline, and good judgment.

Proverbs 23:23

MONTH:_____

	MON	TUE	WED	THU	FRI	SAT	SUN
WEEK 1							
WEEK 2							
WEEK 3							
WEEK 4							
WEEK 5							

TO TO LIST	NOTES

PROJECT PLANNER

PROJECT TITLE:

OBJECTIVES:

START DATE: . . . .

DEADLINE: . . . .

TASK LIST   DUE DATE

☐ . . . .

☐ . . . .

☐ . . . .

☐ . . . .

☐ . . . .

NOTES

Week Of: _____

Sunday

_____ _____
_____ _____
_____ _____
_____ _____
_____

Monday

_____ _____
_____ _____
_____ _____
_____ _____
_____

Tuesday

_____ _____
_____ _____
_____ _____
_____ _____
_____

Wednesday

_____ _____
_____ _____
_____ _____
_____ _____
_____

Positive Affirmation:_____
_____
_____

Thursday

Friday

Saturday

Notes

Week Of: _____

Sunday

_____   _____
_____   _____
_____   _____
_____   _____
_____   _____

Monday

_____   _____
_____   _____
_____   _____
_____   _____
_____   _____

Tuesday

_____   _____
_____   _____
_____   _____
_____   _____
_____   _____

Wednesday

_____   _____
_____   _____
_____   _____
_____   _____
_____   _____

Positive Affirmation:_____
_____
_____

Thursday

Friday

Saturday

Notes

Week Of: _____

Sunday
_____   _____
_____   _____
_____   _____
_____   _____
_____   _____

Monday
_____   _____
_____   _____
_____   _____
_____   _____
_____   _____

Tuesday
_____   _____
_____   _____
_____   _____
_____   _____
_____   _____

Wednesday
_____   _____
_____   _____
_____   _____
_____   _____
_____   _____

Positive Affirmation:_____
_____
_____

Thursday

_____   _____
_____   _____
_____   _____
_____   _____
_____   _____

Friday

_____   _____
_____   _____
_____   _____
_____   _____
_____   _____

Saturday

_____   _____
_____   _____
_____   _____
_____   _____
_____   _____

Notes

_____   _____
_____   _____
_____   _____
_____   _____
_____   _____

Week Of: _____

Sunday

_____ _____
_____ _____
_____ _____
_____ _____
_____ _____

Monday

_____ _____
_____ _____
_____ _____
_____ _____
_____ _____

Tuesday

_____ _____
_____ _____
_____ _____
_____ _____
_____ _____

Wednesday

_____ _____
_____ _____
_____ _____
_____ _____
_____ _____

Positive Affirmation:_____
_____
_____

Thursday

Friday

Saturday

Notes

Think about what I am saying. The Lord will help you understand all these things.

2 Timothy 2:7

MONTH:_____

	MON	TUE	WED	THU	FRI	SAT	SUN
WEEK 1							
WEEK 2							
WEEK 3							
WEEK 4							
WEEK 5							

TO TO LIST	NOTES

PROJECT PLANNER

PROJECT TITLE:

OBJECTIVES:

START DATE: . . . .

DEADLINE: . . . .

TASK LIST   DUE DATE

☐ . . . .

☐ . . . .

☐ . . . .

☐ . . . .

☐ . . . .

NOTES

_____

_____

_____

_____

_____

_____

_____

Week Of: _____

Sunday

_____   _____
_____   _____
_____   _____
_____   _____
_____   _____

Monday

_____   _____
_____   _____
_____   _____
_____   _____
_____   _____

Tuesday

_____   _____
_____   _____
_____   _____
_____   _____
_____   _____

Wednesday

_____   _____
_____   _____
_____   _____
_____   _____
_____   _____

Positive Affirmation:_____
_____
_____

Thursday

Friday

Saturday

Notes

Week Of: _____

Sunday

_____   _____
_____   _____
_____   _____
_____   _____
_____   _____

Monday

_____   _____
_____   _____
_____   _____
_____   _____
_____   _____

Tuesday

_____   _____
_____   _____
_____   _____
_____   _____
_____   _____

Wednesday

_____   _____
_____   _____
_____   _____
_____   _____
_____   _____

Positive Affirmation:_____
_____
_____

Thursday

_____   _____
_____   _____
_____   _____
_____   _____
_____   _____

Friday

_____   _____
_____   _____
_____   _____
_____   _____
_____   _____

Saturday

_____   _____
_____   _____
_____   _____
_____   _____

Notes

_____   _____
_____   _____
_____   _____
_____   _____

Week Of: _____

Sunday

_____ _____
_____ _____
_____ _____
_____ _____
_____ _____

Monday

_____ _____
_____ _____
_____ _____
_____ _____
_____ _____

Tuesday

_____ _____
_____ _____
_____ _____
_____ _____
_____ _____

Wednesday

_____ _____
_____ _____
_____ _____
_____ _____
_____ _____

Positive Affirmation:_____
_____
_____

Thursday

Friday

Saturday

Notes

Week Of: _____

Sunday

_____ _____
_____ _____
_____ _____
_____ _____
_____ _____

Monday

_____ _____
_____ _____
_____ _____
_____ _____
_____ _____

Tuesday

_____ _____
_____ _____
_____ _____
_____ _____
_____ _____

Wednesday

_____ _____
_____ _____
_____ _____
_____ _____
_____

Positive Affirmation:_____
_____
_____

Thursday

_____   _____
_____   _____
_____   _____
_____   _____
_____   _____

Friday

_____   _____
_____   _____
_____   _____
_____   _____
_____   _____

Saturday

_____   _____
_____   _____
_____   _____
_____   _____
_____   _____

Notes

_____   _____
_____   _____
_____   _____
_____   _____
_____   _____

Study this Book of Instruction continually. Meditate on it day and night so you will be sure to obey everything written in it. Only then will you prosper and succeed in all you do.
Joshua 1:8

MONTH:_____

	MON	TUE	WED	THU	FRI	SAT	SUN
WEEK 1							
WEEK 2							
WEEK 3							
WEEK 4							
WEEK 5							

TO TO LIST	NOTES

PROJECT PLANNER

PROJECT TITLE:

OBJECTIVES:

START DATE: . . . .

DEADLINE: . . . .

TASK LIST   DUE DATE

☐ . . . .

☐ . . . .

☐ . . . .

☐ . . . .

☐ . . . .

NOTES

Week Of: _____

Sunday

_____ _____
_____ _____
_____ _____
_____ _____
_____ _____

Monday

_____ _____
_____ _____
_____ _____
_____ _____
_____ _____

Tuesday

_____ _____
_____ _____
_____ _____
_____ _____
_____ _____

Wednesday

_____ _____
_____ _____
_____ _____
_____ _____
_____ _____

Positive Affirmation:_____
_____
_____

Thursday

_____   _____
_____   _____
_____   _____
_____   _____
_____   _____

Friday

_____   _____
_____   _____
_____   _____
_____   _____
_____   _____

Saturday

_____   _____
_____   _____
_____   _____
_____   _____

Notes

_____   _____
_____   _____
_____   _____
_____   _____

Week Of: _____

Sunday

_____   _____
_____   _____
_____   _____
_____   _____
_____   _____

Monday

_____   _____
_____   _____
_____   _____
_____   _____
_____   _____

Tuesday

_____   _____
_____   _____
_____   _____
_____   _____
_____   _____

Wednesday

_____   _____
_____   _____
_____   _____
_____   _____
_____   _____

Positive Affirmation:_____
_____
_____

Thursday

_____   _____
_____   _____
_____   _____
_____   _____
_____   _____

Friday

_____   _____
_____   _____
_____   _____
_____   _____
_____   _____

Saturday

_____   _____
_____   _____
_____   _____
_____   _____
_____   _____

Notes

_____   _____
_____   _____
_____   _____
_____   _____

Week Of: _____

Sunday

_____ _____
_____ _____
_____ _____
_____ _____
_____ _____

Monday

_____ _____
_____ _____
_____ _____
_____ _____
_____ _____

Tuesday

_____ _____
_____ _____
_____ _____
_____ _____
_____ _____

Wednesday

_____ _____
_____ _____
_____ _____
_____ _____

Positive Affirmation:_____
_____
_____

Thursday

Friday

Saturday

Notes

Week Of: _____

Sunday

_____   _____
_____   _____
_____   _____
_____   _____
_____   _____

Monday

_____   _____
_____   _____
_____   _____
_____   _____
_____   _____

Tuesday

_____   _____
_____   _____
_____   _____
_____   _____
_____   _____

Wednesday

_____   _____
_____   _____
_____   _____
_____   _____
_____   _____

Positive Affirmation:_____
_____
_____

Thursday

Friday

Saturday

Notes

For I can do everything through Christ, who gives me strength.   *Philippians 4:13*

MONTH:_____

	MON	TUE	WED	THU	FRI	SAT	SUN
WEEK 1							
WEEK 2							
WEEK 3							
WEEK 4							
WEEK 5							

TO TO LIST	NOTES

PROJECT PLANNER

PROJECT TITLE:

OBJECTIVES:

START DATE: . . . .

DEADLINE: . . . .

TASK LIST   DUE DATE

☐ . . . .

☐ . . . .

☐ . . . .

☐ . . . .

☐ . . . .

NOTES

Week Of: _____

Sunday

_____ _____
_____ _____
_____ _____
_____ _____
_____ _____

Monday

_____ _____
_____ _____
_____ _____
_____ _____
_____ _____

Tuesday

_____ _____
_____ _____
_____ _____
_____ _____
_____ _____

Wednesday

_____ _____
_____ _____
_____ _____
_____ _____
_____ _____

Positive Affirmation:_____
_____
_____

Thursday

_____   _____
_____   _____
_____   _____
_____   _____
_____   _____

Friday

_____   _____
_____   _____
_____   _____
_____   _____
_____   _____

Saturday

_____   _____
_____   _____
_____   _____
_____   _____
_____   _____

Notes

_____   _____
_____   _____
_____   _____
_____   _____
_____   _____

Week Of: _____

Sunday

_____ _____
_____ _____
_____ _____
_____ _____
_____ _____

Monday

_____ _____
_____ _____
_____ _____
_____ _____
_____ _____

Tuesday

_____ _____
_____ _____
_____ _____
_____ _____
_____ _____

Wednesday

_____ _____
_____ _____
_____ _____
_____ _____
_____ _____

Positive Affirmation:_____
_____
_____

Thursday

Friday

Saturday

Notes

Week Of: _____

Sunday

_____   _____
_____   _____
_____   _____
_____   _____
_____   _____

Monday

_____   _____
_____   _____
_____   _____
_____   _____
_____   _____

Tuesday

_____   _____
_____   _____
_____   _____
_____   _____
_____   _____

Wednesday

_____   _____
_____   _____
_____   _____
_____   _____
_____   _____

Positive Affirmation:_____
_____
_____

Thursday

Friday

Saturday

Notes

Week Of: _____

Sunday

_____   _____
_____   _____
_____   _____
_____   _____
_____

Monday

_____   _____
_____   _____
_____   _____
_____   _____
_____

Tuesday

_____   _____
_____   _____
_____   _____
_____   _____
_____

Wednesday

_____   _____
_____   _____
_____   _____
_____   _____
_____

Positive Affirmation:_____
_____
_____

Thursday

Friday

Saturday

Notes

But as for you, be strong and courageous, for your work will be rewarded.

2 Chronicles 15:7

MONTH:_____

	MON	TUE	WED	THU	FRI	SAT	SUN
WEEK 1							
WEEK 2							
WEEK 3							
WEEK 4							
WEEK 5							

TO TO LIST

NOTES

PROJECT PLANNER

PROJECT TITLE:

OBJECTIVES:

START DATE: . . . .

DEADLINE: . . . .

TASK LIST   DUE DATE

☐ . . . .

☐ . . . .

☐ . . . .

☐ . . . .

☐ . . . .

NOTES

_____

_____

_____

_____

_____

_____

_____

Week Of: _____

Sunday

_____ _____
_____ _____
_____ _____
_____ _____
_____ _____

Monday

_____ _____
_____ _____
_____ _____
_____ _____
_____ _____

Tuesday

_____ _____
_____ _____
_____ _____
_____ _____
_____ _____

Wednesday

_____ _____
_____ _____
_____ _____
_____ _____
_____ _____

Positive Affirmation:_____

_____

_____

Thursday

Friday

Saturday

Notes

Week Of: _____

Sunday

_____ _____
_____ _____
_____ _____
_____ _____
_____ _____

Monday

_____ _____
_____ _____
_____ _____
_____ _____
_____ _____

Tuesday

_____ _____
_____ _____
_____ _____
_____ _____
_____ _____

Wednesday

_____ _____
_____ _____
_____ _____
_____ _____
_____ _____

Positive Affirmation:_____
_____
_____

Thursday

_____   _____
_____   _____
_____   _____
_____   _____
_____   _____

Friday

_____   _____
_____   _____
_____   _____
_____   _____
_____   _____

Saturday

_____   _____
_____   _____
_____   _____
_____   _____
_____   _____

Notes

_____   _____
_____   _____
_____   _____
_____   _____
_____   _____

Week Of: _____

Sunday

_____ _____
_____ _____
_____ _____
_____ _____
_____ _____

Monday

_____ _____
_____ _____
_____ _____
_____ _____
_____ _____

Tuesday

_____ _____
_____ _____
_____ _____
_____ _____
_____ _____

Wednesday

_____ _____
_____ _____
_____ _____
_____ _____
_____ _____

Positive Affirmation:_____

_____

_____

Thursday

Friday

Saturday

Notes

Week Of: _____

Sunday

_____   _____
_____   _____
_____   _____
_____   _____
_____   _____

Monday

_____   _____
_____   _____
_____   _____
_____   _____
_____   _____

Tuesday

_____   _____
_____   _____
_____   _____
_____   _____
_____   _____

Wednesday

_____   _____
_____   _____
_____   _____
_____   _____

Positive Affirmation:_____
_____
_____

Thursday

_____   _____
_____   _____
_____   _____
_____   _____
_____   _____

Friday

_____   _____
_____   _____
_____   _____
_____   _____
_____   _____

Saturday

_____   _____
_____   _____
_____   _____
_____   _____
_____   _____

Notes

_____   _____
_____   _____
_____   _____
_____   _____
_____   _____

And we know that God causes everything to work together for the good of those who love God and care called according to His purpose for them.

Romans 8:28

MONTH:_____

	MON	TUE	WED	THU	FRI	SAT	SUN
WEEK 1							
WEEK 2							
WEEK 3							
WEEK 4							
WEEK 5							

TO TO LIST

NOTES

PROJECT PLANNER

PROJECT TITLE:

OBJECTIVES:

START DATE: . . . .

DEADLINE: . . . .

TASK LIST   DUE DATE

☐ . . . .

☐ . . . .

☐ . . . .

☐ . . . .

☐ . . . .

NOTES

_____

_____

_____

_____

_____

_____

_____

Week Of: _____

Sunday

_____   _____
_____   _____
_____   _____
_____   _____
_____   _____

Monday

_____   _____
_____   _____
_____   _____
_____   _____
_____   _____

Tuesday

_____   _____
_____   _____
_____   _____
_____   _____
_____   _____

Wednesday

_____   _____
_____   _____
_____   _____
_____   _____
_____   _____

Positive Affirmation:_____
_____
_____

Thursday

_____   _____
_____   _____
_____   _____
_____   _____
_____   _____

Friday

_____   _____
_____   _____
_____   _____
_____   _____
_____   _____

Saturday

_____   _____
_____   _____
_____   _____
_____   _____
_____   _____

Notes

_____   _____
_____   _____
_____   _____
_____   _____
_____   _____

Week Of: _____

Sunday

_____ _____
_____ _____
_____ _____
_____ _____
_____ _____

Monday

_____ _____
_____ _____
_____ _____
_____ _____
_____ _____

Tuesday

_____ _____
_____ _____
_____ _____
_____ _____
_____ _____

Wednesday

_____ _____
_____ _____
_____ _____
_____ _____
_____

Positive Affirmation:_____

_____

_____

Thursday

_____ _____
_____ _____
_____ _____
_____ _____
_____ _____

Friday

_____ _____
_____ _____
_____ _____
_____ _____
_____ _____

Saturday

_____ _____
_____ _____
_____ _____
_____ _____
_____ _____

Notes

_____ _____
_____ _____
_____ _____
_____ _____
_____ _____

Week Of: _____

Sunday
_____   _____
_____   _____
_____   _____
_____   _____
_____   _____

Monday
_____   _____
_____   _____
_____   _____
_____   _____
_____   _____

Tuesday
_____   _____
_____   _____
_____   _____
_____   _____
_____   _____

Wednesday
_____   _____
_____   _____
_____   _____
_____   _____
_____   _____

Positive Affirmation:_____
_____
_____

Thursday

_____   _____
_____   _____
_____   _____
_____   _____
_____   _____

Friday

_____   _____
_____   _____
_____   _____
_____   _____
_____   _____

Saturday

_____   _____
_____   _____
_____   _____
_____   _____
_____   _____

Notes

_____   _____
_____   _____
_____   _____
_____   _____
_____   _____

Week Of: _____

Sunday

_____ _____
_____ _____
_____ _____
_____ _____
_____ _____

Monday

_____ _____
_____ _____
_____ _____
_____ _____
_____ _____

Tuesday

_____ _____
_____ _____
_____ _____
_____ _____
_____ _____

Wednesday

_____ _____
_____ _____
_____ _____
_____ _____

Positive Affirmation:_____
_____
_____

Thursday

_____   _____
_____   _____
_____   _____
_____   _____
_____   _____

Friday

_____   _____
_____   _____
_____   _____
_____   _____
_____   _____

Saturday

_____   _____
_____   _____
_____   _____
_____   _____
_____   _____

Notes

_____   _____
_____   _____
_____   _____
_____   _____
_____   _____

Tune your ears to wisdom, and concentrate on understanding.

Proverbs 2:2

M O N T H : _ _ _ _ _ _ _ _ _ _ _

	MON	TUE	WED	THU	FRI	SAT	SUN
WEEK 1							
WEEK 2							
WEEK 3							
WEEK 4							
WEEK 5							

TO TO LIST

NOTES

PROJECT PLANNER

PROJECT TITLE:

OBJECTIVES:

START DATE: . . . .

DEADLINE: . . . .

TASK LIST   DUE DATE

☐ . . . .

☐ . . . .

☐ . . . .

☐ . . . .

☐ . . . .

NOTES

Week Of: _____

Sunday

_____   _____
_____   _____
_____   _____
_____   _____
_____   _____

Monday

_____   _____
_____   _____
_____   _____
_____   _____
_____   _____

Tuesday

_____   _____
_____   _____
_____   _____
_____   _____
_____   _____

Wednesday

_____   _____
_____   _____
_____   _____
_____   _____

Positive Affirmation:_____
_____
_____

Thursday

_____   _____
_____   _____
_____   _____
_____   _____
_____   _____

Friday

_____   _____
_____   _____
_____   _____
_____   _____
_____   _____

Saturday

_____   _____
_____   _____
_____   _____
_____   _____
_____   _____

Notes

_____   _____
_____   _____
_____   _____
_____   _____

Week Of: _____

Sunday

_____ _____
_____ _____
_____ _____
_____ _____
_____ _____
_____ _____

Monday

_____ _____
_____ _____
_____ _____
_____ _____
_____ _____

Tuesday

_____ _____
_____ _____
_____ _____
_____ _____
_____ _____

Wednesday

_____ _____
_____ _____
_____ _____
_____ _____

Positive Affirmation:_____
_____
_____

Thursday

Friday

Saturday

Notes

Week Of: _____

Sunday

_____ _____
_____ _____
_____ _____
_____ _____
_____ _____

Monday

_____ _____
_____ _____
_____ _____
_____ _____
_____ _____

Tuesday

_____ _____
_____ _____
_____ _____
_____ _____
_____ _____

Wednesday

_____ _____
_____ _____
_____ _____
_____ _____
_____ _____

Positive Affirmation:_____
_____
_____

Thursday

Friday

Saturday

Notes

Week Of: _____

Sunday

_____ _____
_____ _____
_____ _____
_____ _____
_____ _____

Monday

_____ _____
_____ _____
_____ _____
_____ _____
_____ _____

Tuesday

_____ _____
_____ _____
_____ _____
_____ _____
_____ _____

Wednesday

_____ _____
_____ _____
_____ _____
_____ _____
_____ _____

Positive Affirmation:_____
_____
_____

Thursday

_____   _____
_____   _____
_____   _____
_____   _____
_____   _____

Friday

_____   _____
_____   _____
_____   _____
_____   _____
_____   _____

Saturday

_____   _____
_____   _____
_____   _____
_____   _____
_____   _____

Notes

_____   _____
_____   _____
_____   _____
_____   _____

Work hard so you can present yourself to God and receive His approval. Be a good worker, one who does not need to be ashamed and who correctly explains the word of truth.

2 Timothy 2:15

MONTH:_____

	MON	TUE	WED	THU	FRI	SAT	SUN
WEEK 1							
WEEK 2							
WEEK 3							
WEEK 4							
WEEK 5							

TO TO LIST	NOTES

PROJECT PLANNER

PROJECT TITLE:

OBJECTIVES:

START DATE: . . . .

DEADLINE: . . . .

TASK LIST   DUE DATE

☐ . . . .

☐ . . . .

☐ . . . .

☐ . . . .

☐ . . . .

NOTES

_____

_____

_____

_____

_____

_____

_____

Week Of: _____

Sunday

_____ _____
_____ _____
_____ _____
_____ _____
_____ _____

Monday

_____ _____
_____ _____
_____ _____
_____ _____
_____ _____

Tuesday

_____ _____
_____ _____
_____ _____
_____ _____
_____ _____

Wednesday

_____ _____
_____ _____
_____ _____
_____ _____
_____ _____

Positive Affirmation:_____
_____
_____

Thursday

Friday

Saturday

Notes

Week Of: _____

Sunday

_____ _____
_____ _____
_____ _____
_____ _____
_____ _____

Monday

_____ _____
_____ _____
_____ _____
_____ _____
_____ _____

Tuesday

_____ _____
_____ _____
_____ _____
_____ _____
_____ _____

Wednesday

_____ _____
_____ _____
_____ _____
_____ _____
_____ _____

Positive Affirmation:_____
_____
_____

Thursday

Friday

Saturday

Notes

Week Of: _____

Sunday

_____   _____
_____   _____
_____   _____
_____   _____
_____   _____

Monday

_____   _____
_____   _____
_____   _____
_____   _____
_____   _____

Tuesday

_____   _____
_____   _____
_____   _____
_____   _____
_____   _____

Wednesday

_____   _____
_____   _____
_____   _____
_____   _____
_____   _____

Positive Affirmation:_____
_____
_____

Thursday

Friday

Saturday

Notes

Week Of: _____

Sunday

_____   _____
_____   _____
_____   _____
_____   _____
_____   _____

Monday

_____   _____
_____   _____
_____   _____
_____   _____
_____   _____

Tuesday

_____   _____
_____   _____
_____   _____
_____   _____
_____   _____

Wednesday

_____   _____
_____   _____
_____   _____
_____   _____
_____   _____

Positive Affirmation:_____
_____
_____

Thursday

_____   _____
_____   _____
_____   _____
_____   _____
_____   _____

Friday

_____   _____
_____   _____
_____   _____
_____   _____
_____   _____

Saturday

_____   _____
_____   _____
_____   _____
_____   _____
_____   _____

Notes

_____   _____
_____   _____
_____   _____
_____   _____

The Lord of Heaven's Armies is a wonderful teacher, and He gives the farmer great wisdom.

Isaiah 28:28

MONTH:_____

	MON	TUE	WED	THU	FRI	SAT	SUN
WEEK 1							
WEEK 2							
WEEK 3							
WEEK 4							
WEEK 5							

TO TO LIST	NOTES

PROJECT PLANNER

PROJECT TITLE:

OBJECTIVES:

START DATE: . . . .

DEADLINE: . . . .

TASK LIST   DUE DATE

☐ . . . .

☐ . . . .

☐ . . . .

☐ . . . .

☐ . . . .

NOTES

Week Of: _____

Sunday

_____ _____
_____ _____
_____ _____
_____ _____
_____ _____

Monday

_____ _____
_____ _____
_____ _____
_____ _____
_____ _____

Tuesday

_____ _____
_____ _____
_____ _____
_____ _____
_____ _____

Wednesday

_____ _____
_____ _____
_____ _____
_____ _____
_____ _____

Positive Affirmation:_____
_____
_____

Thursday

Friday

Saturday

Notes

Week Of: _____

Sunday

_____ _____
_____ _____
_____ _____
_____ _____
_____ _____

Monday

_____ _____
_____ _____
_____ _____
_____ _____
_____ _____

Tuesday

_____ _____
_____ _____
_____ _____
_____ _____
_____ _____

Wednesday

_____ _____
_____ _____
_____ _____
_____ _____
_____ _____

Positive Affirmation:_____
_____
_____

Thursday

Friday

Saturday

Notes

Week Of: _____

Sunday

_____ _____
_____ _____
_____ _____
_____ _____
_____ _____

Monday

_____ _____
_____ _____
_____ _____
_____ _____
_____ _____

Tuesday

_____ _____
_____ _____
_____ _____
_____ _____
_____ _____

Wednesday

_____ _____
_____ _____
_____ _____
_____ _____
_____ _____

Positive Affirmation:_____
_____
_____

Thursday

Friday

Saturday

Notes

Week Of: _____

Sunday

_____ _____
_____ _____
_____ _____
_____ _____
_____ _____

Monday

_____ _____
_____ _____
_____ _____
_____ _____
_____ _____

Tuesday

_____ _____
_____ _____
_____ _____
_____ _____
_____ _____

Wednesday

_____ _____
_____ _____
_____ _____
_____ _____
_____ _____

Positive Affirmation:_____
_____
_____

Thursday

_____ _____
_____ _____
_____ _____
_____ _____
_____ _____

Friday

_____ _____
_____ _____
_____ _____
_____ _____
_____ _____

Saturday

_____ _____
_____ _____
_____ _____
_____ _____
_____ _____

Notes

_____ _____
_____ _____
_____ _____
_____ _____
_____ _____

CONTACTS

Name
Phone
Email
Website
Address
Notes

Name
Phone
Email
Website
Address
Notes

Name
Phone
Email
Website
Address
Notes

Name
Phone
Email
Website
Address
Notes

Name
Phone
Email
Website
Address
Notes

Name
Phone
Email
Website
Address
Notes

Name
Phone
Email
Website
Address
Notes

Name
Phone
Email
Website
Address
Notes

Name
Phone
Email
Website
Address
Notes

Name
Phone
Email
Website
Address
Notes

CONTACTS

♟ Name

☎ Phone

✉ Email

🌐 Website

● Address

🗎 Notes

♟ Name

☎ Phone

✉ Email

🌐 Website

● Address

🗎 Notes

♟ Name

☎ Phone

✉ Email

🌐 Website

● Address

🗎 Notes

♟ Name

☎ Phone

✉ Email

🌐 Website

● Address

🗎 Notes

♟ Name

☎ Phone

✉ Email

🌐 Website

● Address

🗎 Notes

♟ Name

☎ Phone

✉ Email

🌐 Website

● Address

🗎 Notes

♟ Name

☎ Phone

✉ Email

🌐 Website

● Address

🗎 Notes

♟ Name

☎ Phone

✉ Email

🌐 Website

● Address

🗎 Notes

♟ Name

☎ Phone

✉ Email

🌐 Website

● Address

🗎 Notes

♟ Name

☎ Phone

✉ Email

🌐 Website

● Address

🗎 Notes

♟ Name

☎ Phone

✉ Email

🌐 Website

● Address

🗎 Notes

♟ Name

☎ Phone

✉ Email

🌐 Website

● Address

🗎 Notes

NOTES

NOTES

NOTES